STEM IN OUR WORLD

MEDICAL TECHNOLOGY

GENOMICS, GROWING ORGANS, AND MORE

BY JOHN WOOD

Gareth Stevens PUBLISHING

Please visit our website, www.garethstevens.com.

For a free color catalog of all our high-quality books,
call toll free 1-800-542-2595 or fax 1-877-542-2596.

Cataloging-in-Publication Data

Names: Wood, John.
Title: Medical technology: genomics, growing organs, and more / John Wood.
Description: New York : Gareth Stevens Publishing, 2019. | Series: STEM in our world | Includes glossary and index.
Identifiers: LCCN ISBN 9781538226476 (pbk.) | ISBN 9781538226469 (library bound) | ISBN 9781538226483 (6 pack)
Subjects: LCSH: Medical technology--Juvenile literature. | Medical innovations--Juvenile literature.
Classification: LCC R855.4 W663 2019 | DDC 610.1'4--dc23

First Edition

Published in 2019 by
Gareth Stevens Publishing
111 East 14th Street, Suite 349
New York, NY 10003

Produced for Gareth Stevens by Booklife
Writer: John Wood
Editor: Holly Duhig
Designer: Daniel Scase

Printed in the United States of America

CPSIA compliance information: Batch #CS18GS: For further information, contact Gareth Stevens, New York, New York at 1-800-542-2595.

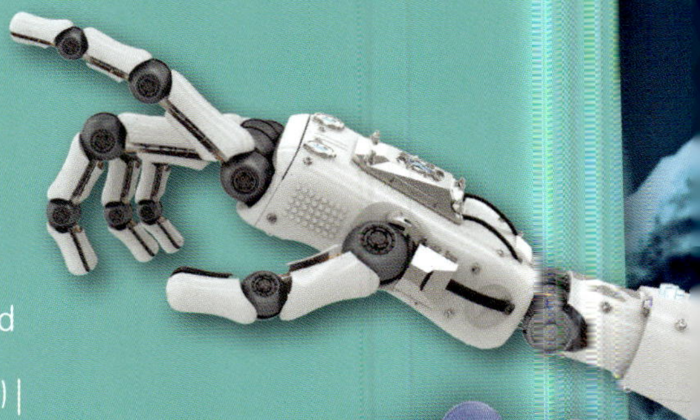

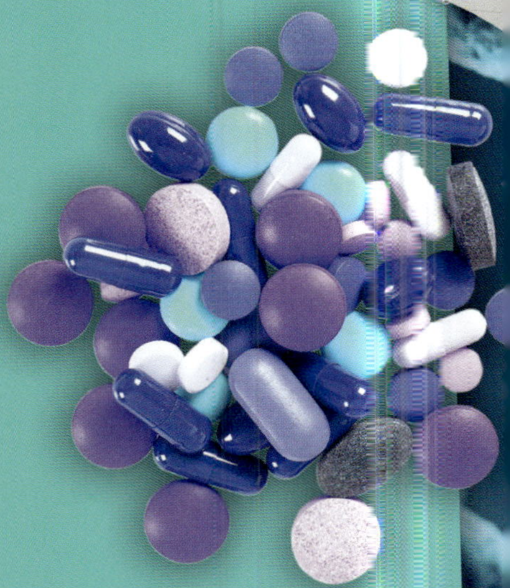

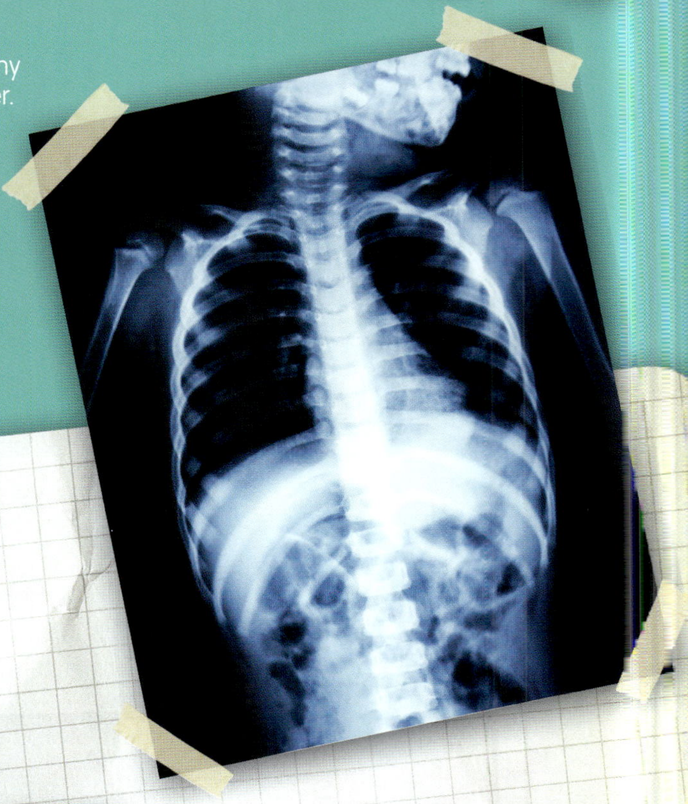

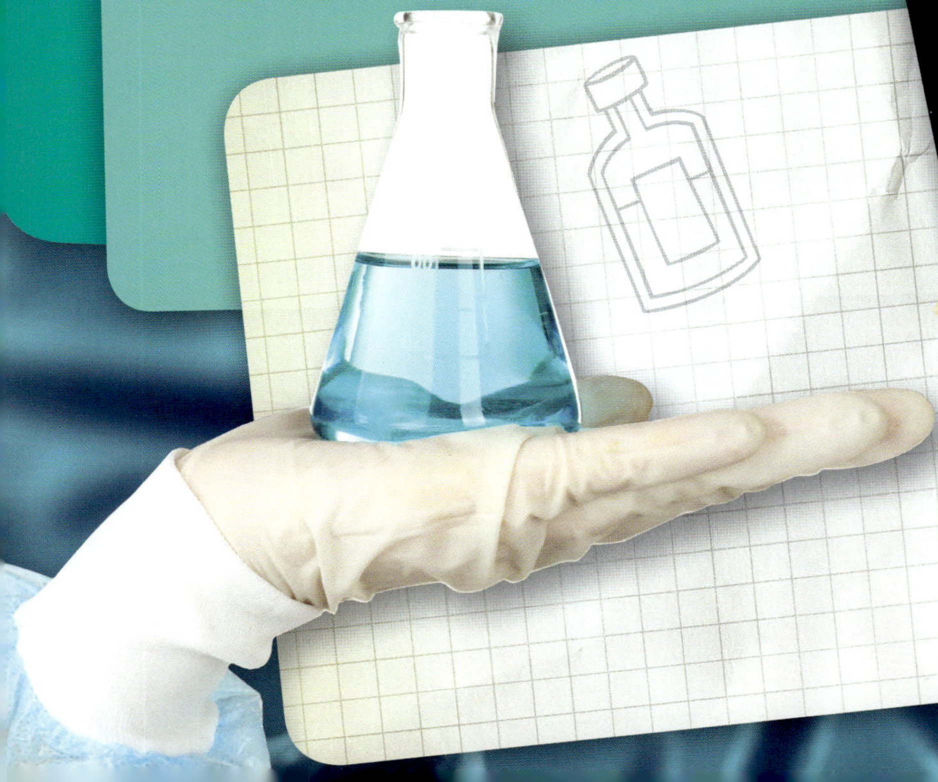

CONTENTS

WORDS THAT LOOK LIKE *THIS* ARE EXPLAINED IN THE GLOSSARY ON PAGE 31.

WELCOME TO STEM SCHOOL

MEET YOUR TEACHER

ATTENTION, STUDENTS. MY NAME IS PROFESSOR TESS TUBE, AND I AM YOUR TEACHER. I'M JUST PUTTING SOME UNIMPORTANT THINGS AWAY.

SSH! NO, NO, NO, DON'T WORRY, STUDENTS. THERE ARE NO TALKING ROBOTS HERE. ANYWAY, THERE IS SOMETHING MUCH MORE EXCITING TO TALK ABOUT. BY PICKING UP THIS BOOK, YOU ARE NOW PART OF STEM SCHOOL. STEM STANDS FOR:

SCIENCE, TECHNOLOGY, ENGINEERING, AND MATH.

BUT STEM ISN'T ALL ABOUT CREATING AN ARMY OF ROBOT SERVANTS. STEM IS IMPORTANT IN ALL SORTS OF WAYS.

WHY IS STEM IMPORTANT IN ALL SORTS OF WAYS?

You can probably find STEM in almost every part of your life. Here are a few examples:

- COMPUTERS AT SCHOOL, WHICH HELP US LEARN
- TOASTERS, KETTLES, AND OVENS AT HOME, WHICH HELP US MAKE FOOD AND DRINK
- HOSPITAL MACHINES AND MEDICINE, WHICH HELP US LIVE LONGER
- CARS, BOATS, AND PLANES, WHICH HELP US TRAVEL AROUND THE WORLD QUICKLY
- WEATHER REPORTS THAT TELL US WHAT THE WEATHER IS GOING TO BE LIKE

STEM is all about understanding and solving problems in the real world. When we have an idea of how something might work, we test it again and again to make sure it is right. Then we can create machines and **SYSTEMS** to solve the problems we have.

Sometimes we get new information, and find out that our old ideas were wrong. But that is OK – STEM subjects are all about changing your ideas based on the information you have.

MAKE NO MISTAKE, STUDENTS, STEM SCHOOL WILL BE TRICKY. IT'S GOING TO TAKE LOTS OF HARD WORK AND HEAD SCRATCHING TO UNDERSTAND HOW EVERYTHING WORKS. SO, LET'S GET OUR THINKING CAPS ON! I'VE GOT MINE RIGHT HERE – THE THINKCAP3000, WHICH INCREASES MY BRAIN POWER BY 68%. OKAY, LET'S SEE WHAT WE WILL BE LEARNING ABOUT TODAY...

STEM AND MEDICINE

Medicine in History

If you went back in time, you would see that medicine used to be very different. There were no clean hospitals or expensive machines like there are today. This was not good for all the people who were ill and injured. However, medical technology has come a long way.

An Injection

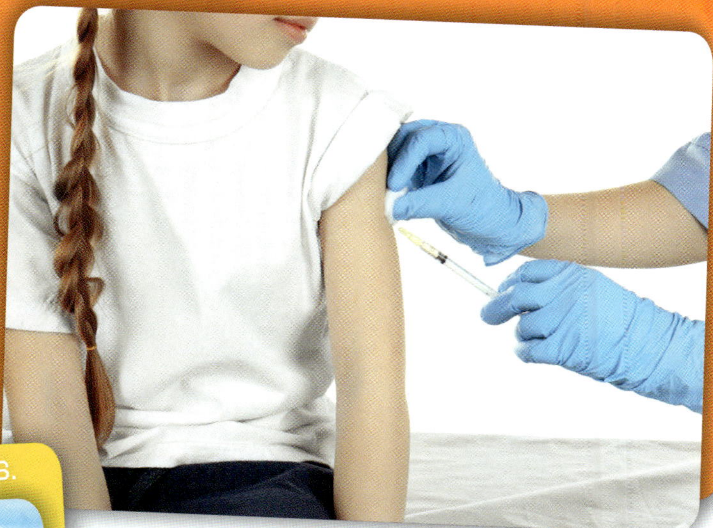

Discoveries That Led to Today's Medicine

At the end of the 18th century, Edward Jenner discovered **VACCINES**, which are injections of less harmful diseases that can prevent much nastier diseases. You might remember having a vaccine because someone sticks a needle in your arm and you have to be really brave!

This **SURGEON** is washing their hands.

At the end of the 19th century, people understood that diseases were caused by germs. This meant that hospitals and medical instruments were kept very clean in order to stop the spread of germs.

In 1928, Alexander Fleming discovered penicillin, which is a type of **ANTIBIOTIC**. Antibiotics help cure bacterial infections. You might have had to take antibiotics at some point in your life.

FLEMING WAS ONE MESSY SCIENTIST! HE DISCOVERED PENICILLIN IN ONE OF HIS MOLDY PETRI DISHES AFTER COMING BACK FROM VACATION!

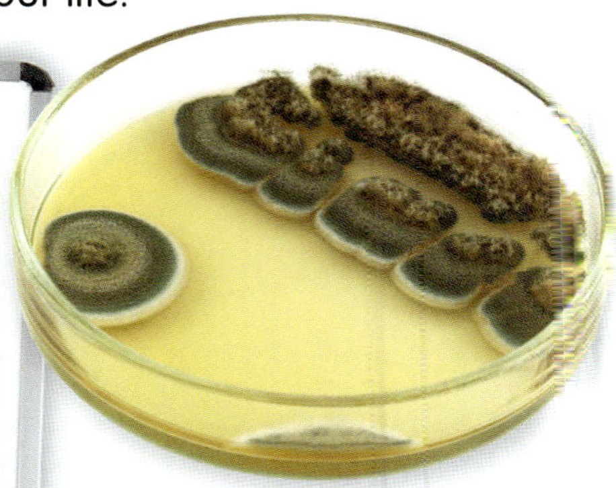

PENICILLIN IN A PETRI DISH

More Research Needed

Although lots of discoveries have been made, there is still a lot to do in medicine. New technology and discoveries could treat injuries faster or cure the deadly diseases that still exist in the world. STEM research into medicine could save many lives.

Many of the world's deadliest diseases affect people in **less economically developed countries** the most. Diseases like malaria cause hundreds of thousands of people to die every year, mostly in African countries. STEM research into medicine can help people all over the world.

AH, THE BELL! IT LOOKS LIKE THE LESSONS ARE ABOUT TO BEGIN. ROLL UP YOUR SLEEVES, STUDENTS, WE ARE GOING TO TAKE A LOOK AT STEM IN ACTION. LET'S TURN THE PAGE AND GET YOUR FIRST LESSON STARTED...

X-RAYS

DIFFERENT TYPES OF LIGHT

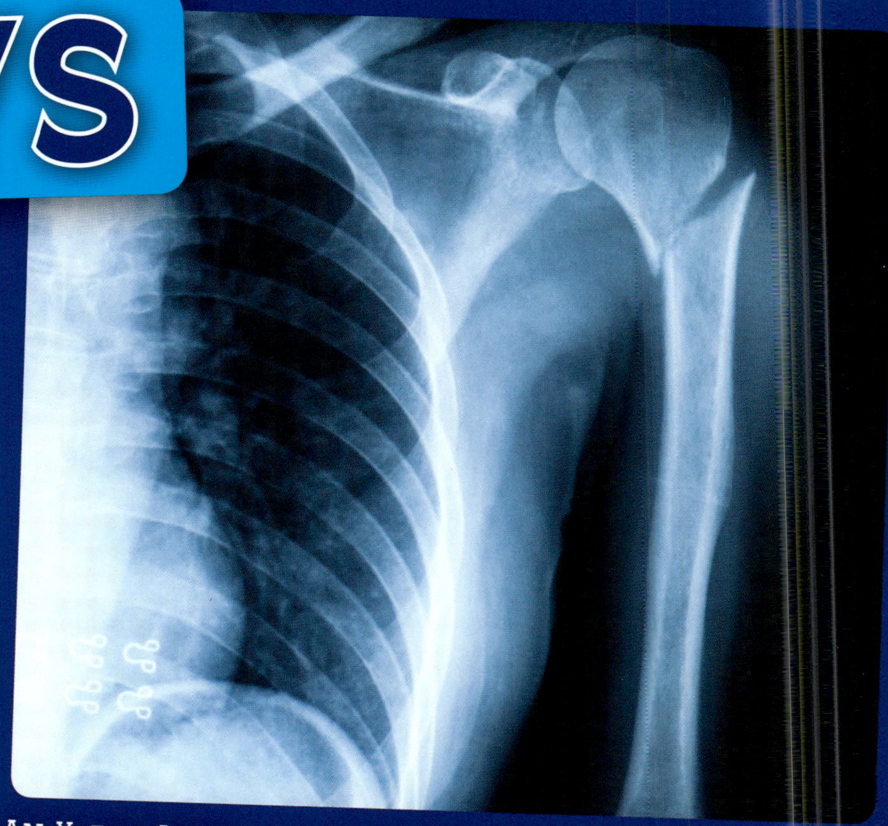

AN X-RAY SCAN

Doctors use X-rays to see through skin and ***TISSUE*** and look at bones and teeth. X-rays are a type of light. But it is not like the light that you see from the sun or a light bulb.

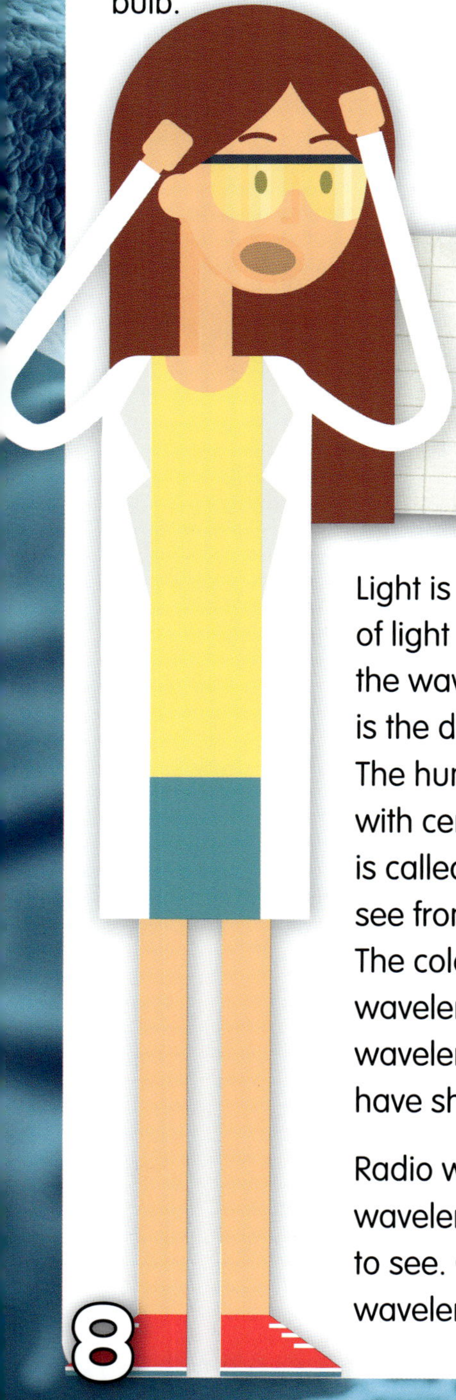

THAT'S RIGHT! I'M ABOUT TO BLOW YOUR MIND, SO GET READY. NOT ALL LIGHT CAN BE SEEN BY HUMANS! SOME OF IT IS INVISIBLE TO US.

Light is a wave of ***ENERGY***. A wave of light has a wavelength, just like the waves in the sea. A wavelength is the distance between each wave. The human eye can only see light with certain wavelengths. This light is called visible light, which we see from lightbulbs and the sun. The color of light depends on its wavelength. Red light has a longer wavelength. Blue and violet light have shorter wavelengths.

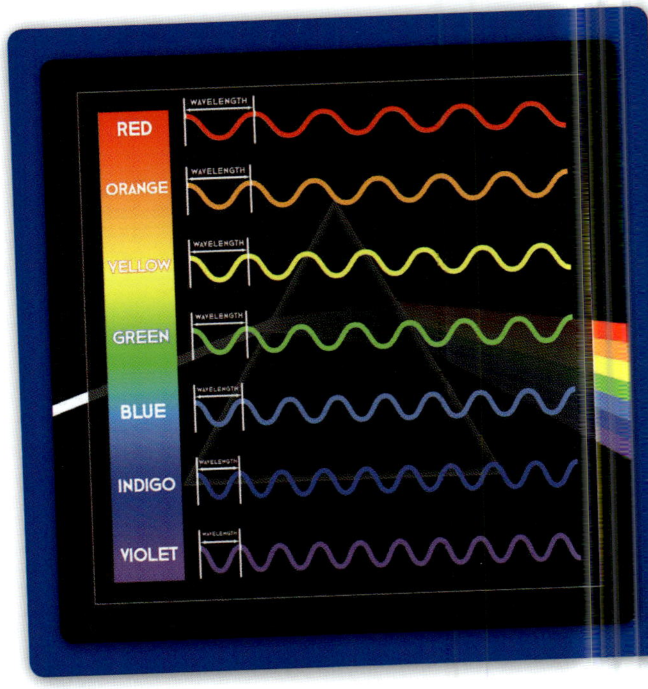

Radio waves and microwaves have wavelengths that are too long for us to see. Gamma rays and X-rays have wavelengths that are too short for us to see.

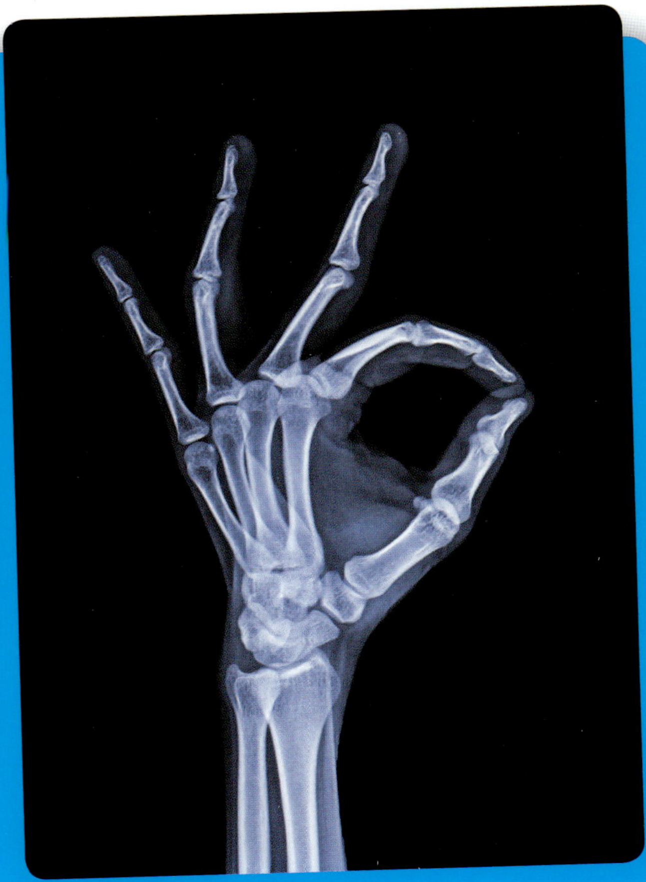

X-rays are used because of their short wavelengths and high energy. This allows them to pass through materials which would block visible light.

How Do X-ray Scans Work?

X-rays are fired through a patient and onto a piece of film or a digital **SENSOR**. X-rays pass right through skin and tissue, but are blocked by things like bones and teeth. The X-rays that pass through are absorbed by the film or sensor at the other end. The parts of the film or sensor which have absorbed X-rays are black, and the parts blocked by bones are white. This creates an image of the skeleton.

Why Do Bones Block X-rays?

Bones block X-rays because they are made of heavier atoms than skin and tissue. Atoms are the basic building blocks of **MATTER**. Everything you can touch is made up of different types of atoms.

Some atoms are heavier than others. The heavier an atom is, the better it is at blocking X-rays. Our skin and tissue are mainly made of light atoms. However, our bones have much heavier atoms.

A Model of an Atom

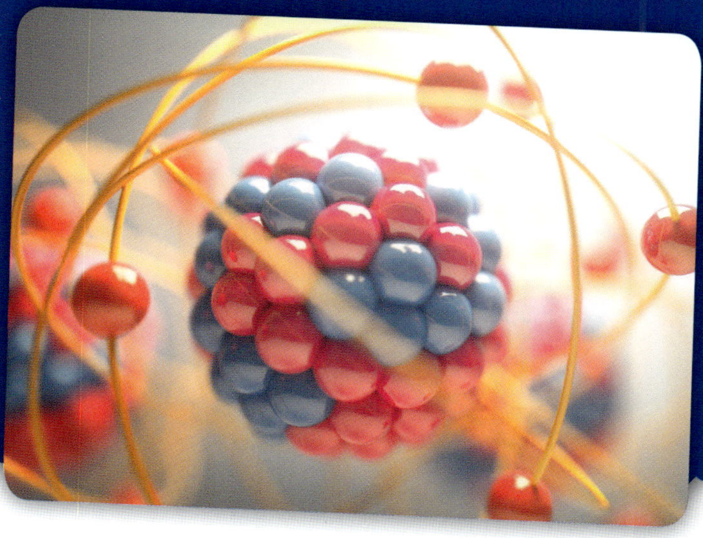

X-RAYS ARE USEFUL FOR LOOKING INSIDE THE BODY FOR BROKEN BONES WITHOUT HAVING TO CUT A PATIENT OPEN.

ROBOT-ASSISTED SURGERY

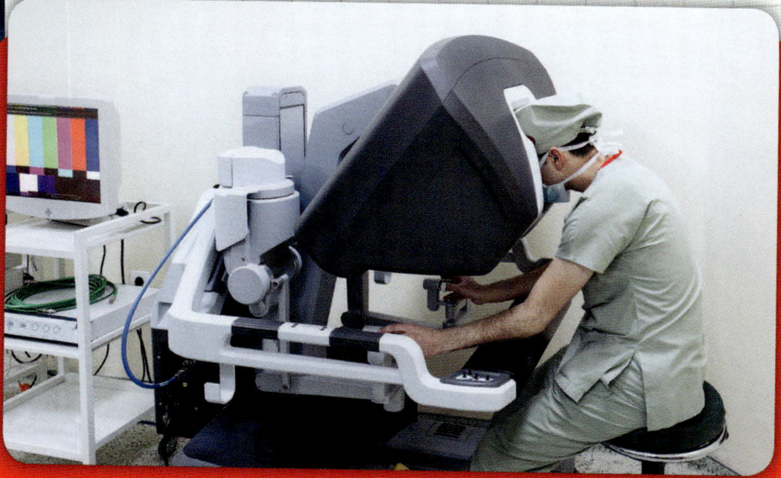

THIS IS THE COMPUTER A SURGEON MIGHT USE FOR ROBOTIC SURGERY.

Hospitals use lots of machines to help make sick people better, but what about using robots? The da Vinci robot is a machine that helps surgeons perform surgery. Instead of using their hands, surgeons can control da Vinci's robotic arms using a computer. The robotic arms can be controlled from hundreds of miles away. This is useful for doctors who don't have time to travel to different hospitals to perform surgery. It also means that doctors could use da Vinci to save somebody's life without ever meeting the patient!

IN A RECENT TEST ON A *VIRTUAL* PATIENT, A SURGEON CONTROLLED THE ROBOT ARMS FROM OVER 1,180 MILES (1,900 KM) AWAY.

The da Vinci robot has four arms. One arm holds a high-quality camera, which allows the surgeon to see the patient. The other three arms hold medical equipment like ***SCALPELS***. The robot also has microphones so the surgeon can speak to anyone in the room.

THIS ROBOT IS PERFORMING SURGERY.

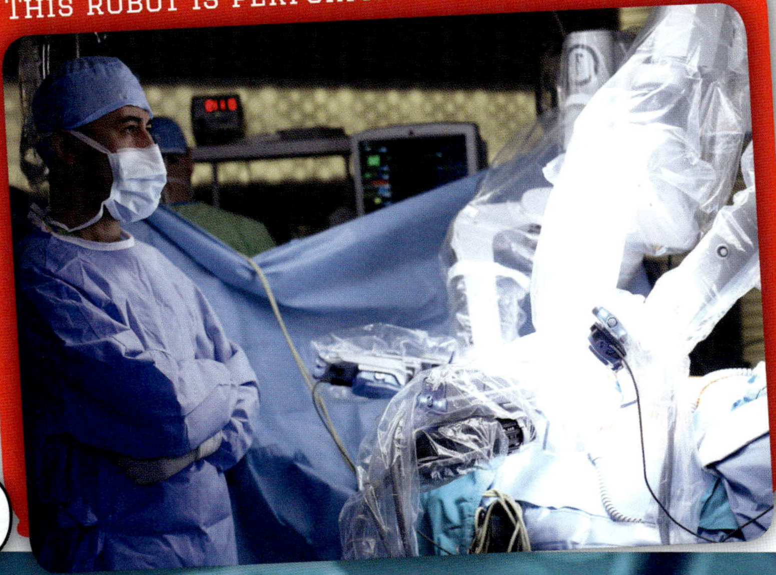

Better Than Surgeons

Surgery can last for many hours. Robots like da Vinci can be useful because they make surgery more comfortable and less tiring for the surgeon. The robot's arms are also able to make neater and smaller cuts than a human can. This helps patients recover faster.

THESE ARE THE SPECIAL CONTROLS A SURGEON USES.

Latency and Money

There are some problems with robot-assisted surgery. It takes a lot of practice. It is also very expensive, so not all hospitals can afford to buy the robots. Sometimes there is also a problem with latency, which is the delay between when the surgeon tells the robot what to do and when the robot does it. This latency gets worse the farther away the surgeon is from da Vinci. For a safe surgery, there needs to be almost no latency.

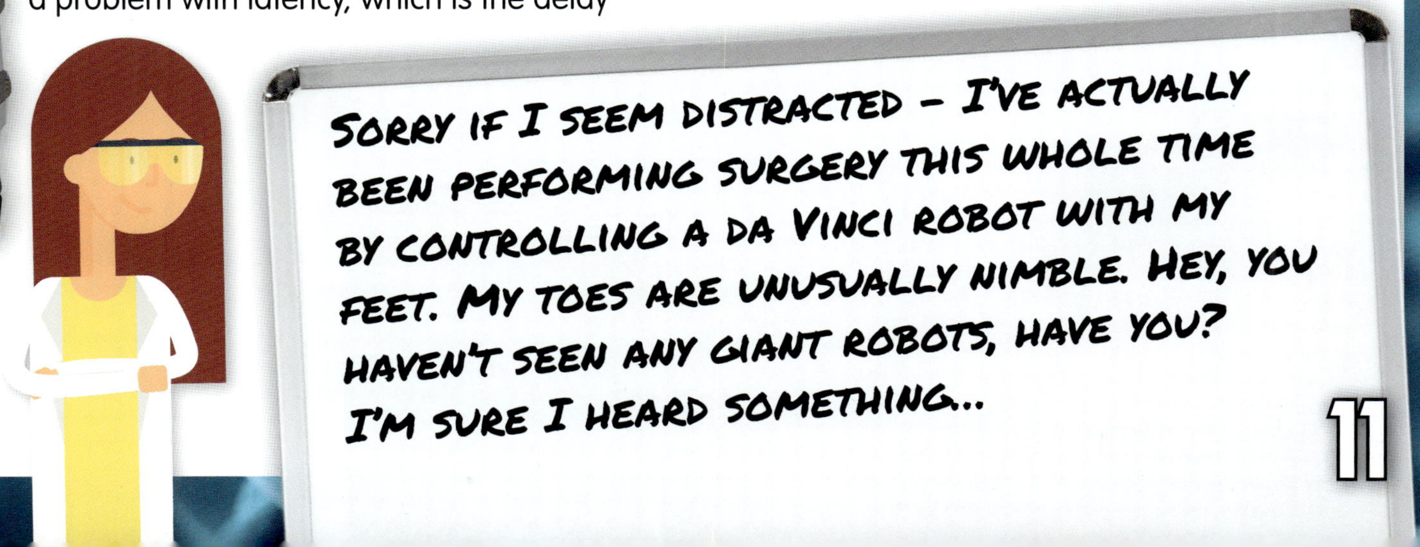

ANESTHETIC

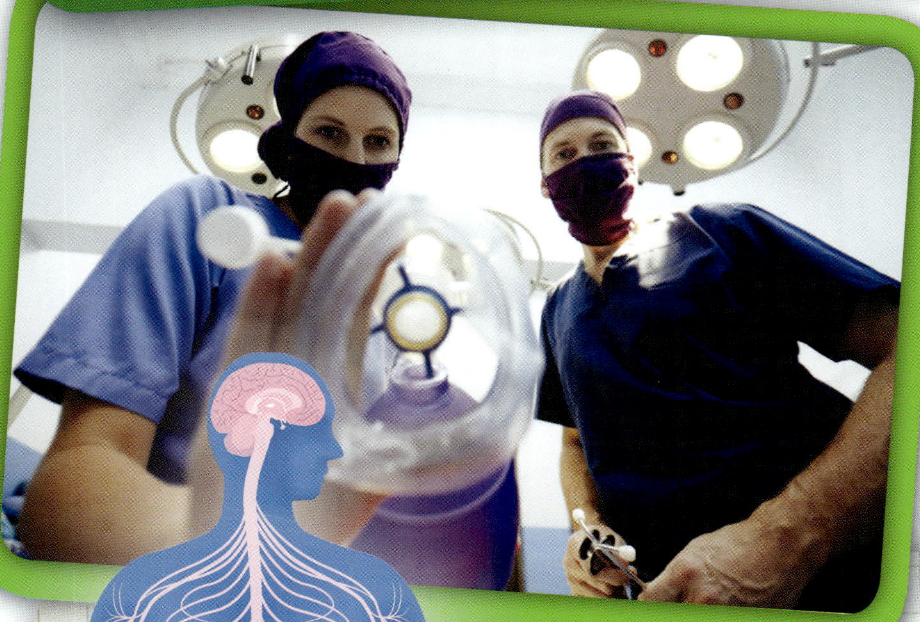

Feeling Woozy

Have you ever been given an injection that makes your mouth go numb at the dentist? Have you ever been put to sleep for a while in the hospital? You might have been given an anesthetic, which is a drug used in medicine to stop you feeling pain.

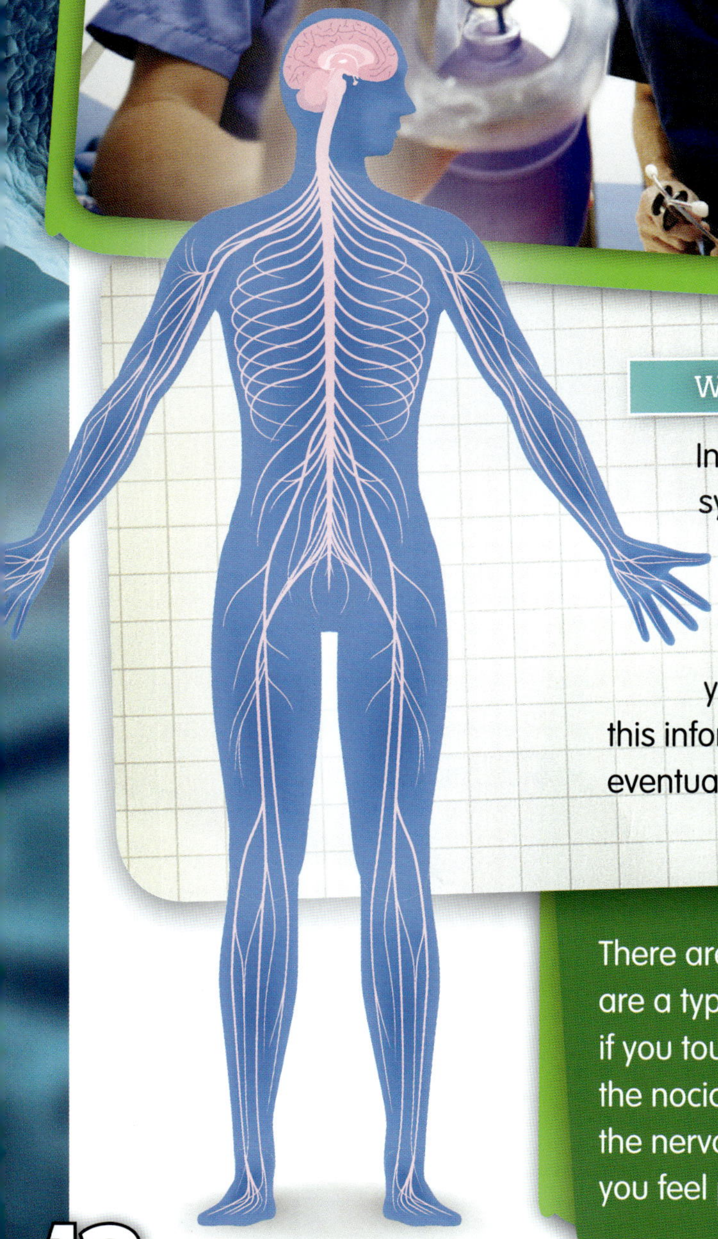

Why Do We Feel Pain?

Information is sent around the body by the nervous system. The nervous system is made up of lots of **NEURONS**. The neurons under your skin are called sensor neurons, because they sense things like temperature and pressure. When you touch something, the sensory neurons carry this information to other neurons, and this information eventually reaches your brain.

There are different types of sensory neurons. Nociceptors are a type of sensory neuron that sense pain. For example, if you touch dangerous **CHEMICALS** or something very hot, the nociceptors send that information to your brain through the nervous system. When the brain gets this information, you feel pain.

There are two types of anesthetic: local anesthetic and general anesthetic.

Local Anesthetic

A local anesthetic is usually injected into a person's skin with a needle. The needle contains a drug that holds onto neurons and stops them from working. This means the nociceptors cannot send any information to the brain, so the brain does not know what is going on in that area of the body. The patient feels no pain, but does not go to sleep when under local anesthetic.

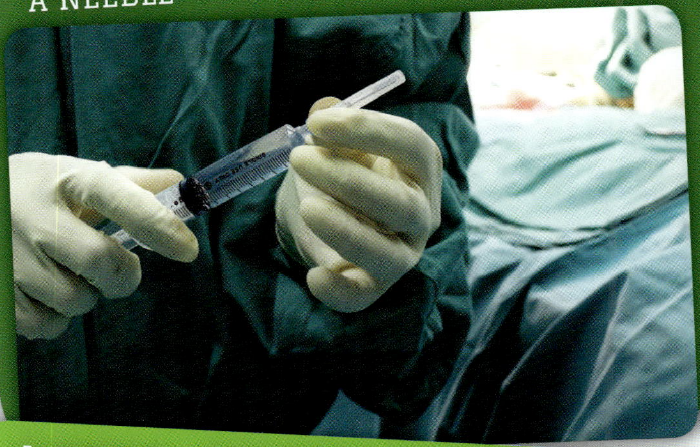

A NEEDLE

General Anesthetic

General anesthetic makes a patient unconscious for a while, which stops them from feeling anything at all. There are many things that can be used as a general anesthetic. A gas called nitrous oxide is often used. Other times, an injection of a mixture of chemicals is used. Being under general anesthetic is like being in an extremely deep sleep.

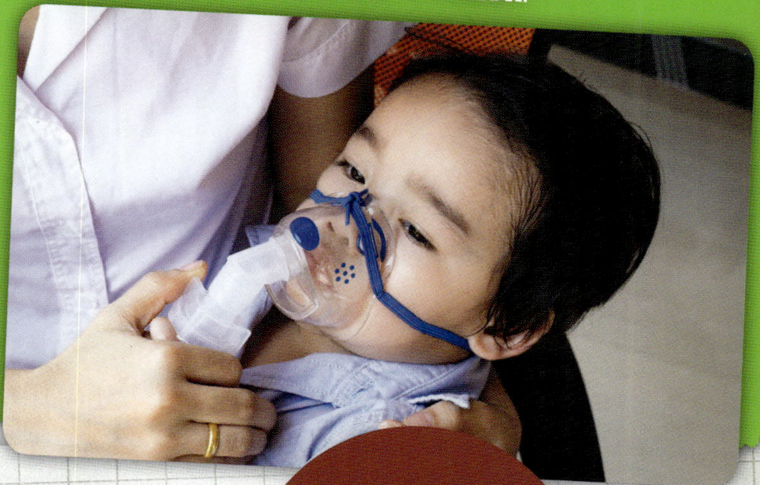

A GENERAL ANESTHETIC IS OFTEN GIVEN TO A PERSON THROUGH A MASK.

ALTHOUGH GENERAL ANESTHETICS ARE SAFE TO USE, NOBODY KNOWS WHY THEY WORK. NOT EVEN PROFESSOR TESS TUBE KNOWS.

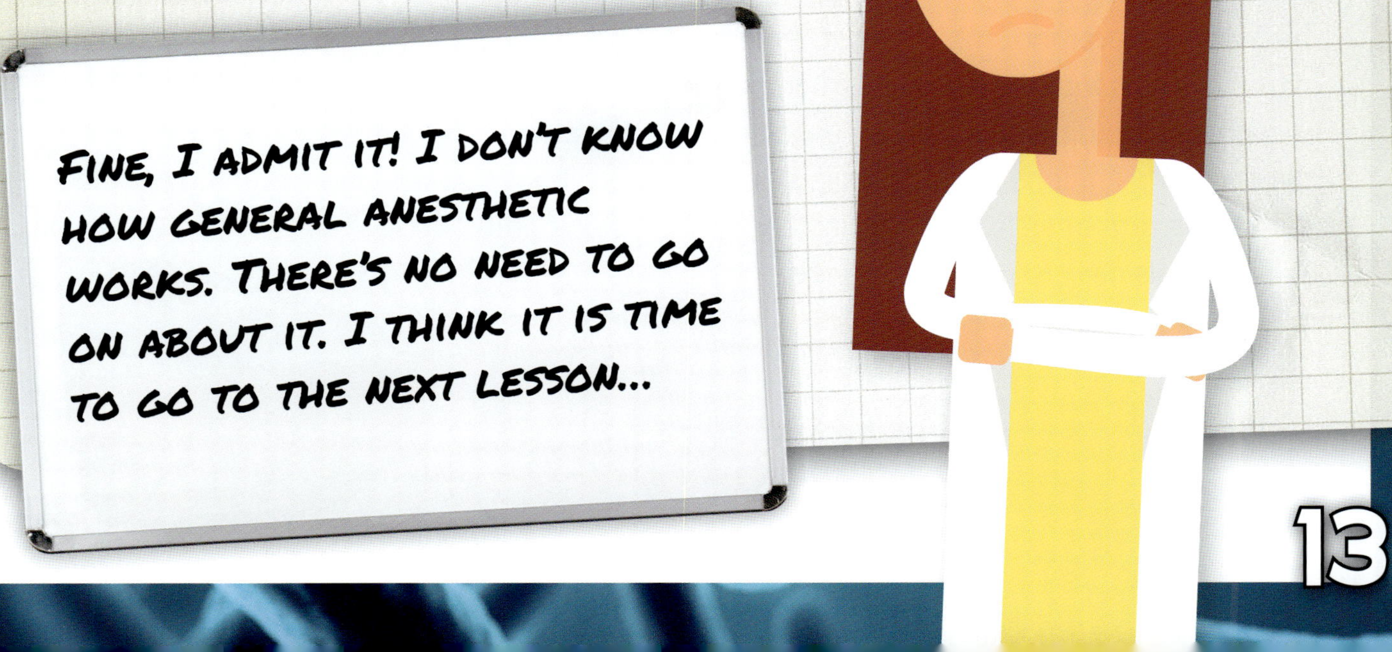

BIONIC LIMBS

From Hook Hands to Robot Hands

This runner is using a prosthetic leg.

A prosthetic is an **artificial** replacement for a missing or broken body part. Wooden legs and glass eyes are prosthetics. A pirate's hook hand is a type of prosthetic, too. But a new type of intelligent, robotic prosthetic is being tested. These are often called bionic **limbs**, or bionics, and can be controlled using the brain.

How Are Bionic Limbs Controlled?

If a person has lost a limb, such as an arm, there will still be neurons connecting the brain to wherever the limb was lost. If these neurons aren't too damaged, they can be reconnected to different muscles, usually in the chest. This means that any brain signal sent to the arm goes to the chest instead. Brain signals are just electrical signals, so **electrodes** can be used to pick up any information from the brain. These electrodes are placed on the chest and then wired to the bionic limb. Now, when the brain sends a signal to the arm, it actually goes to the electrodes on the chest, and then to the bionic limb.

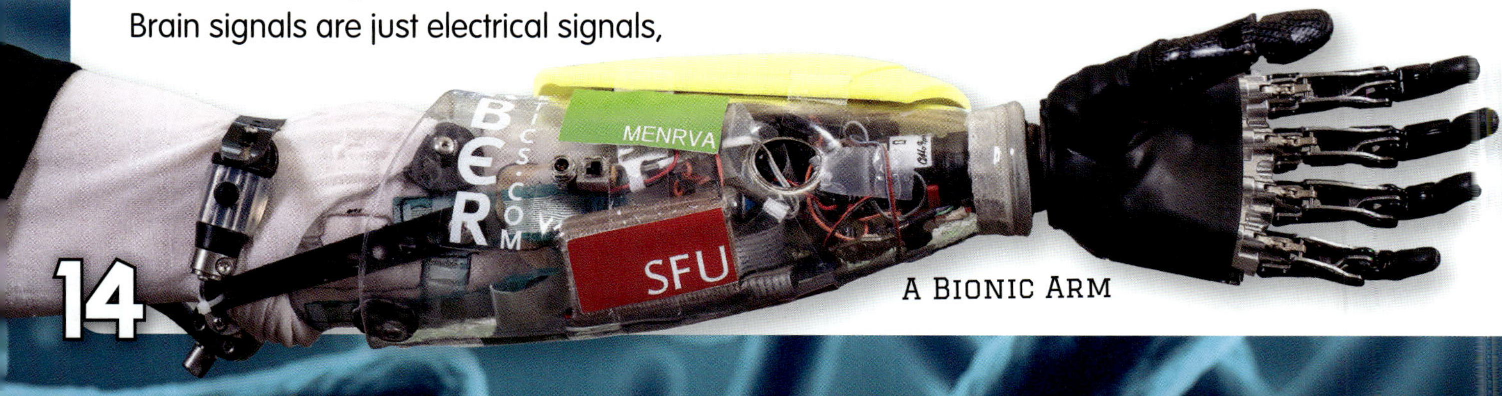

A Bionic Arm

Touchy Robots

There are many different kinds of bionics being tested, such as bionic arms, legs, eyes, and ears. Some bionic arms are even capable of feeling the world around them, like a **biological** arm would. Pressure sensors on the bionic arm are attached to an electrode. Using a computer device kept in the person's pocket, the bionic arm can send signals to the person's sensory neurons, which take that information to the brain. As this technology becomes better and less expensive, bionic limbs might become a lot more common in the future.

OF COURSE, I'VE CREATED MANY BIONIC LIMBS IN MY TIME. THE LAST ROBOTIC ARM I MADE WAS VERY SPECIAL – IT HAD A BUILT-IN TOASTER. UNFORTUNATELY, IT WAS BANNED. SOMETHING ABOUT "BREAKFAST-RELATED ACCIDENTS." NEVER MIND, THERE ARE PLENTY MORE INVENTIONS THAT NEED INVENTING.

DEFIBRILLATORS

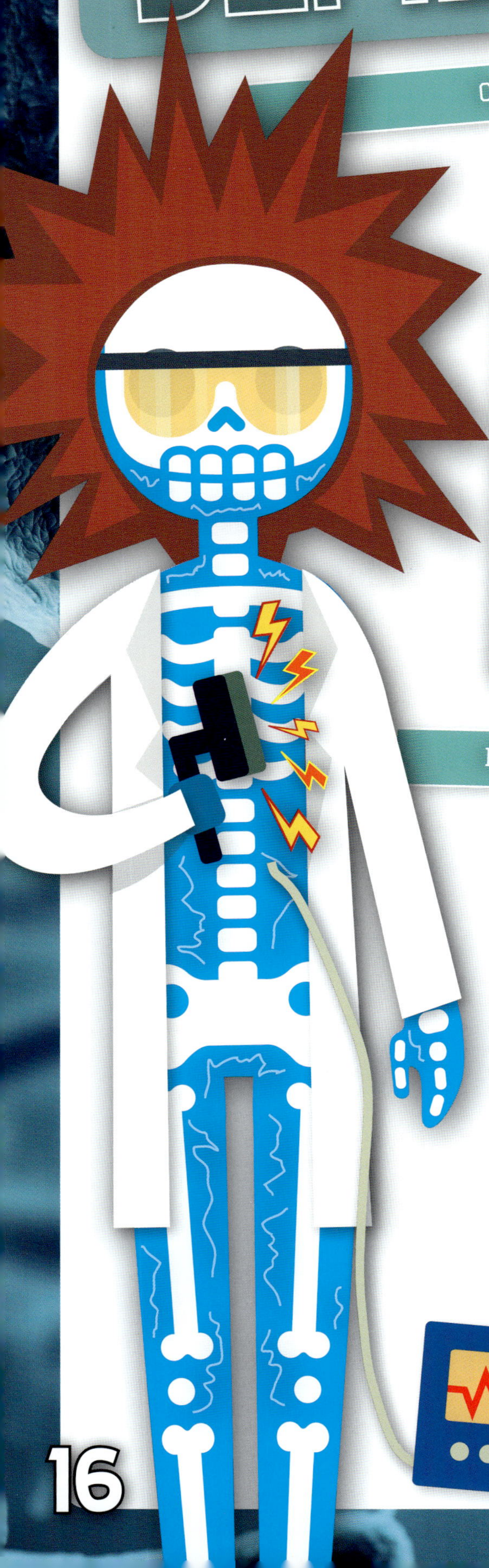

CLEAR!

When a patient's heart isn't working properly, a device called a defibrillator is placed on their chest to zap them with electricity. This may not seem like a good idea if someone is seriously ill, but it can actually save someone's life in certain situations.

OF COURSE, THE PERSON USING THE DEFIBRILLATOR HAS TO BE CAREFUL THAT THEY DON'T TOUCH THE ELECTRIC PART, OTHERWISE THEY WILL ACCIDENTALLY ELECTROCUTE THEMSEL–

AAAAAARRRR GGGGGGHHHH!!!

HOW THE HEART WORKS

The heart has two sides. The right side collects blood from the body and sends it to the lungs to collect oxygen. The left side receives the blood that is now full of oxygen and pumps it out to the rest of the body.

Each side has two **CHAMBERS**. Atriums are chambers which collect the blood, while ventricles are chambers that pump the blood out.

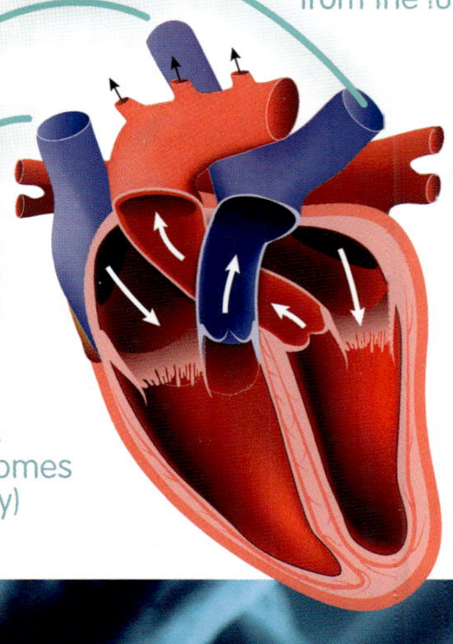

The Sinoatrial Node

The heart's rhythm is controlled by a bunch of neurons in the heart called the sinoatrial node. The sinoatrial node fires electric signals that travel through the **cells** in the heart, causing the different chambers to work together and beat in a steady rhythm. When exercising, scared, excited, or ill, the brain tells the sinoatrial node that the body needs more oxygen from the blood. The electrical signals become quicker, the heart beats faster, and more blood is pumped around the body.

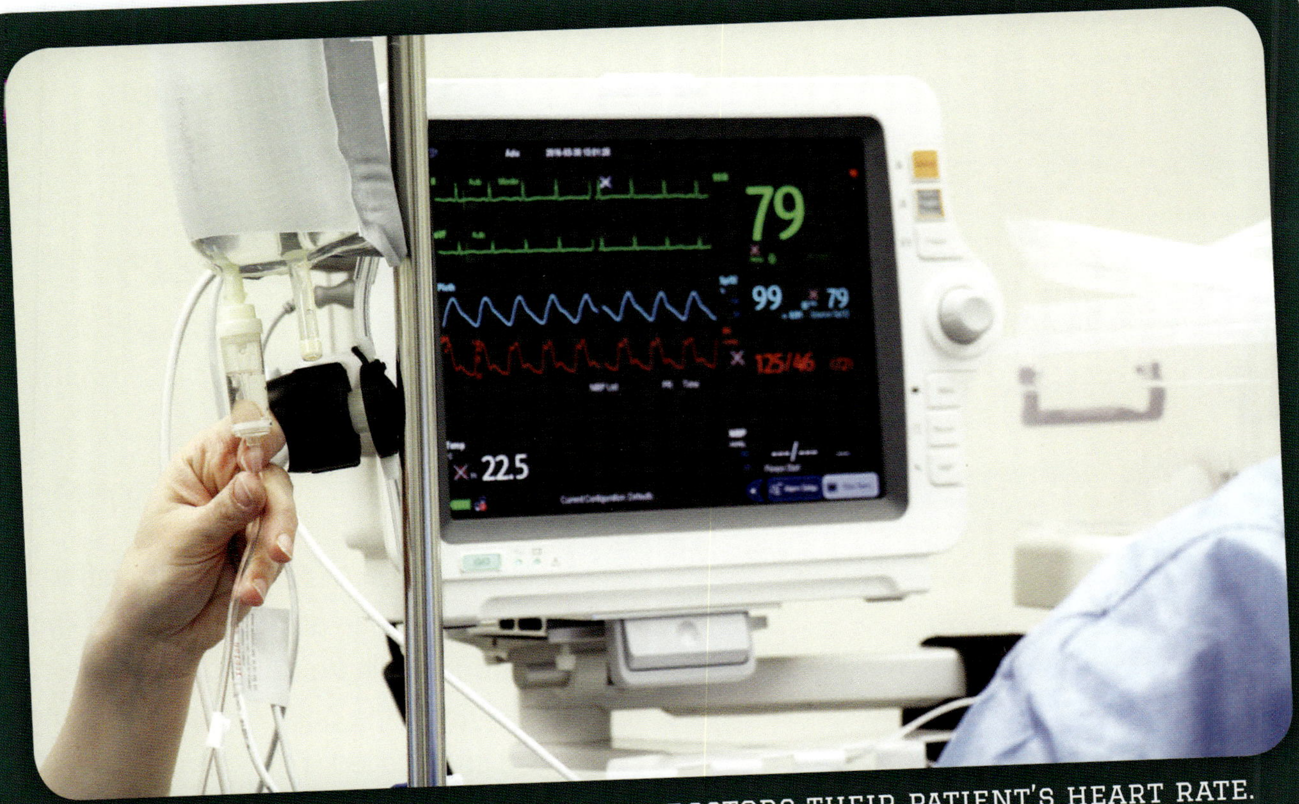

HOSPITALS HAVE MACHINES THAT SHOW DOCTORS THEIR PATIENT'S HEART RATE.

Ventricular Fibrillation

Ventricular fibrillation is a type of heart attack where the sinoatrial node has lost control. Instead of one big electrical impulse from one place, there are lots of weak electrical signals from cells all over the heart. Now the heart isn't beating in a steady rhythm, and the different chambers are not working together. Ventricular fibrillation causes the heart to quiver, and no blood is sent around the body.

Bring in the Defibrillator

Electrodes are attached to the patient's chest and an electric shock is sent through the body. The big electric shock cuts out all the little electrical signals, which lets the sinoatrial node take over again.

DEFIBRILLATOR, ELECTRODES, DUMMY

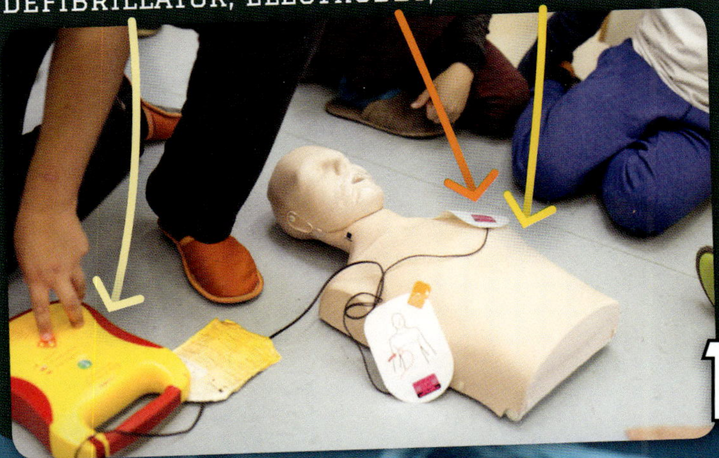

GENOMICS

YOU DON'T KNOW WHAT GENOMICS IS? OH, DON'T WORRY, IT'S JUST THE STUDY OF GENES. YOU DON'T KNOW WHAT GENES ARE? NO SWEAT: GENES ARE JUST COLLECTIONS OF DNA. YOU DON'T KNOW WHAT DNA IS? OK, LET'S START FROM THE BEGINNING...

A DOUBLE HELIX

DNA

DNA is a mixture of different **ACIDS**. These acids pair up in a twisted ladder called a double helix. The order in which the pairs are joined up make a code called a genetic code, which is a set of instructions on how to make a person. Almost every cell in your body contains a set of your DNA. This means that almost every cell in your body carries a set of instructions on how to make you.

GENES

Genes are sections of DNA. Different genes are in charge of different things. Some genes decide the color of your eyes, while other genes are all about how to make your blood cells. Genomics is about understanding and changing genes.

ABOUT 99% OF GENES ARE THE SAME IN ALL PEOPLE, BUT 1% ARE DIFFERENT – THIS IS WHAT MAKES YOU UNIQUE.

The Human Genome Project

The full set of genes for any living thing is called a genome.

In 2003, scientists successfully mapped out and understood what each human gene does. This was called the Human Genome Project, and it took 13 years to complete.

HUMANS HAVE AROUND 20,000 GENES.

People with sickle cell anemia have blood cells shaped like this.

How Does the Human Genome Project Help Medicine?

The project is important for curing genetic diseases, which are diseases that are linked to a person's genes. For example, sickle cell anemia is a genetic disease in which the red blood cells are made in a curved, sickle shape. These sickle blood cells do not last a long time, and can get stuck in the body. This can cause pain for someone with this disease, and make them tired, out of breath, and more at risk from other illnesses.

However, thanks to the human genome project, scientists know which genes are responsible for creating the sickle blood cells. One day they will be able to change those genes so that they make normal, healthy blood cells. So far, this has only been successful in mice, but hopefully this will work in humans in the future.

GROWING ORGANS

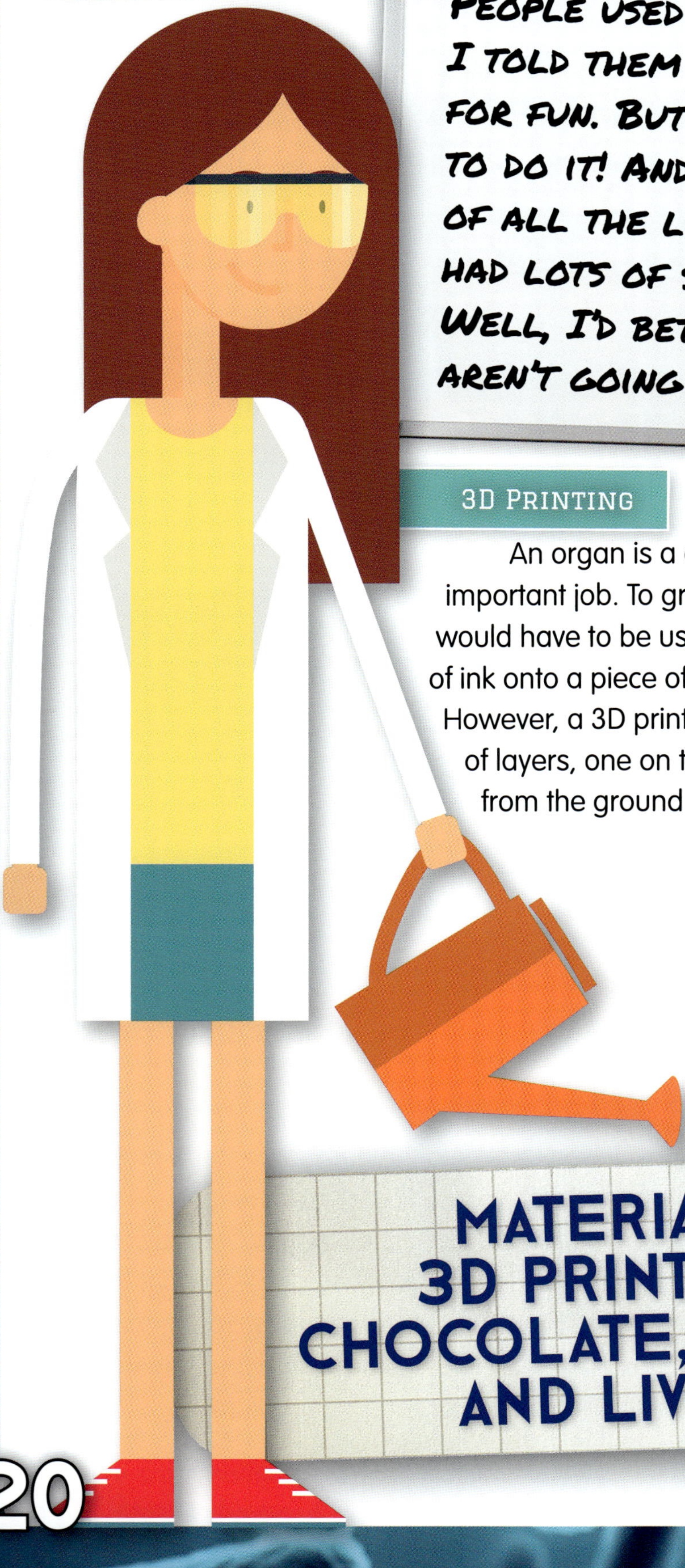

People used to call me crazy when I told them I grow hearts and lungs for fun. But now everybody is trying to do it! And a good thing, too – think of all the lives we could save if we had lots of spare organs lying around. Well, I'd better go – those hearts aren't going to water themselves!

3D Printing

An organ is a certain part of the body which has an important job. To grow an organ, technology called **3D** printing would have to be used. A regular printer prints a layer of ink onto a piece of paper to produce words and images. However, a 3D printer uses all sorts of materials to print lots of layers, one on top of the other. This way, it builds 3D things from the ground up.

A 3D PRINTED WRENCH

MATERIALS USED IN 3D PRINTING INCLUDE CHOCOLATE, PLASTIC, METAL, AND LIVING TISSUE.

Printing Living Tissue

When 3D printing living tissue, cells are usually held together with a **GEL** to keep it in the right shape. The cells then bind together and the gel is washed away. Today, printing living tissue can be used to repair organs and bones. In the future, the printing will hopefully be used to print full organs like hearts and kidneys.

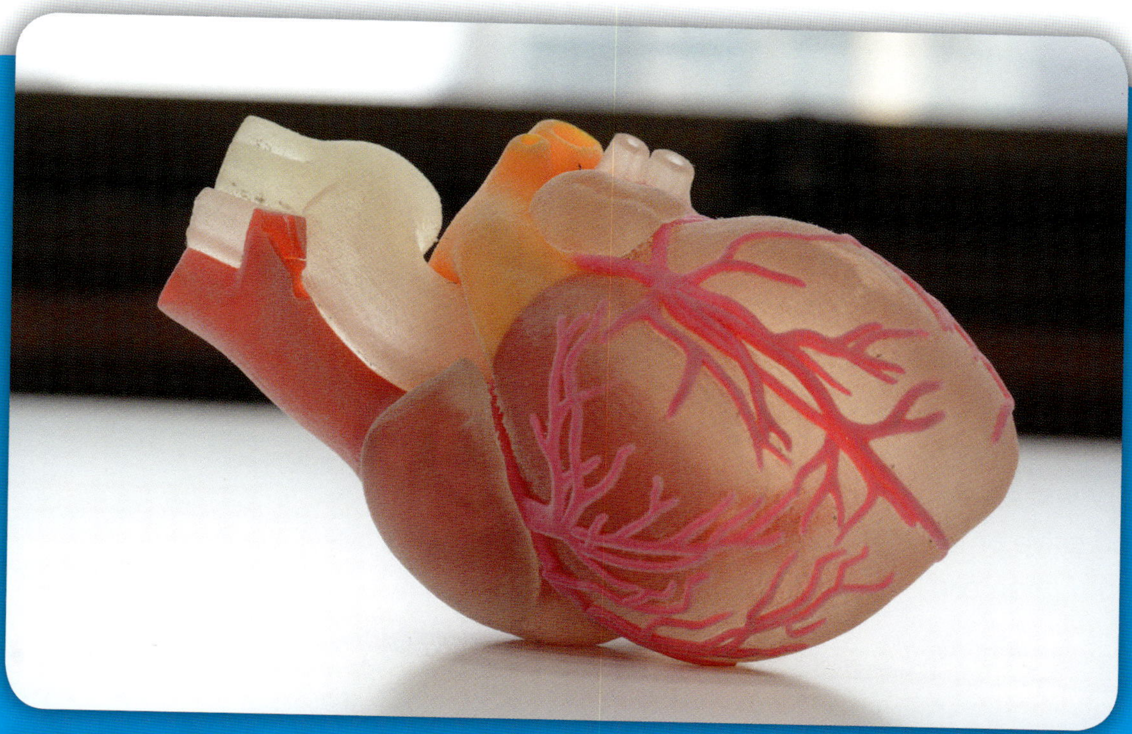

A Plastic Model of a 3D Printed Heart

Organoids

Not all organs are grown to be put in people. Organoids are tiny versions of organs that are grown in a **LABORATORY**. Scientists can do tests on the organoids or infect them with diseases to see how they react. This provides the scientists with useful information about what might happen if a real organ had the disease.

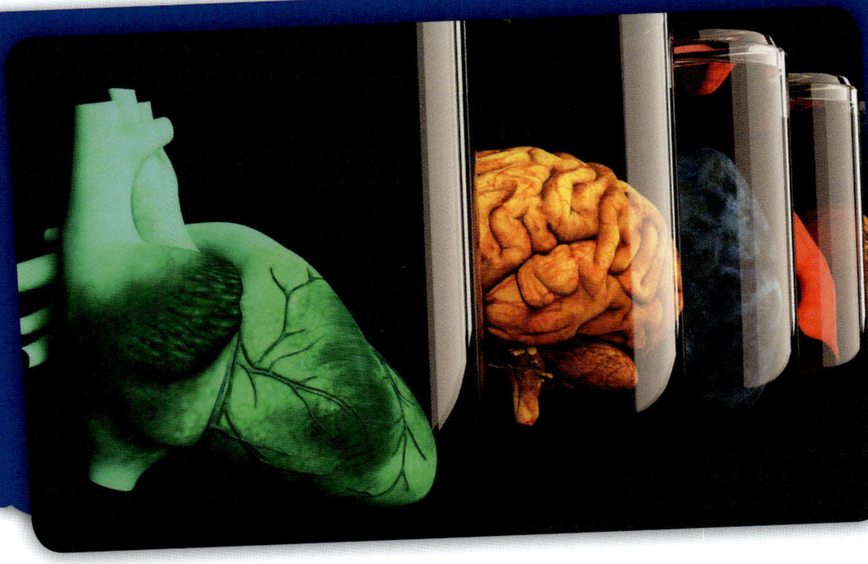

Organoids are grown using stem cells. Stem cells are cells that are able to turn into any other type of cell, so they are very useful to scientists who want to grow body parts like organs.

ARTIFICIAL INTELLIGENCE (AI)

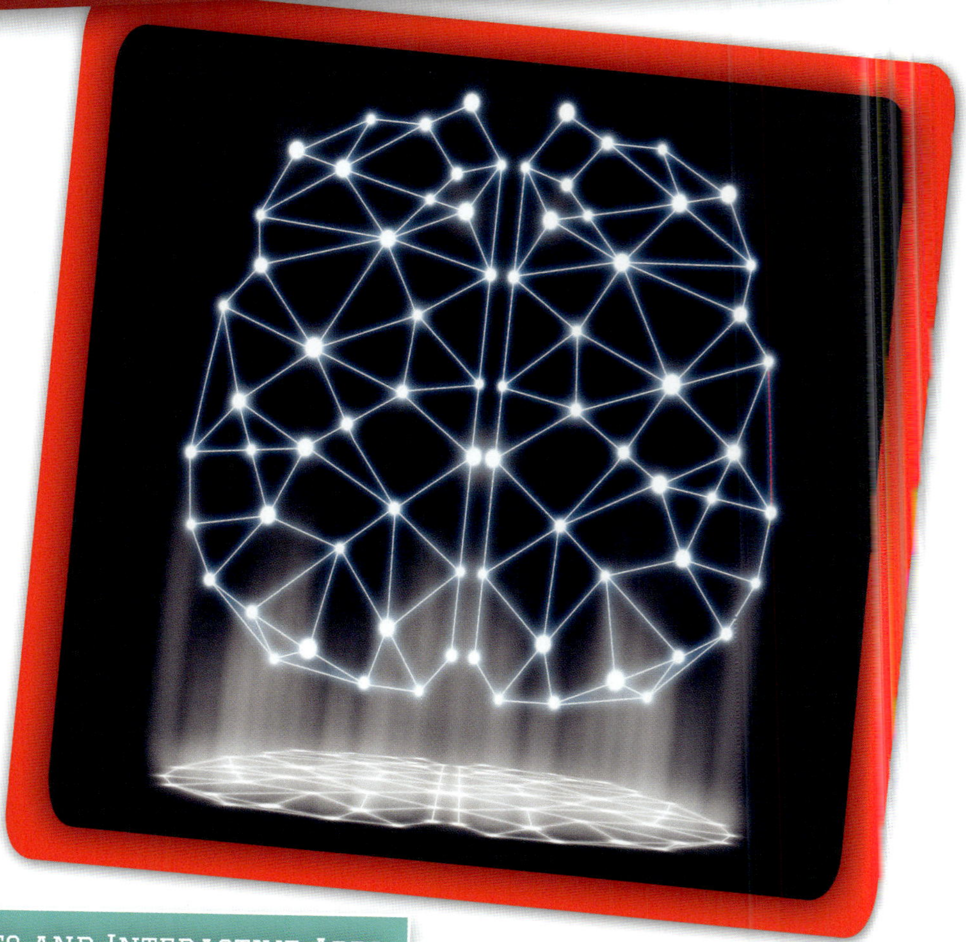

WHAT IS AI?

Most machines are designed to do one task and need to be controlled by a human. However, a machine with artificial intelligence, or AI for short, would be able to make its own decisions and react to the world around it. This would mean that AIs would be able to learn and solve problems just like a human can.

CHATBOTS AND INTERACTIVE APPS

Most phones and computers nowadays have a basic version of AI called chatbots. You can ask your phone's chatbot questions and it will be able to understand your voice and answer them. Probably the most well-known chatbot is called Siri, which is made by a company called Apple. In medicine, chatbots like these are an important part of health apps such as HealthTap, which listens to a person's problems and figures out what is wrong.

ALTHOUGH CHATBOTS ARE VERY SMART AND USEFUL, THEY ARE NOT TRUE AI. MANY OF THEIR RESPONSES ARE PROGRAMMED BY HUMANS.

WATSON

Watson is a supercomputer created by IBM. Watson is going to be a computer doctor. Although not true AI, Watson is one of the best attempts yet.

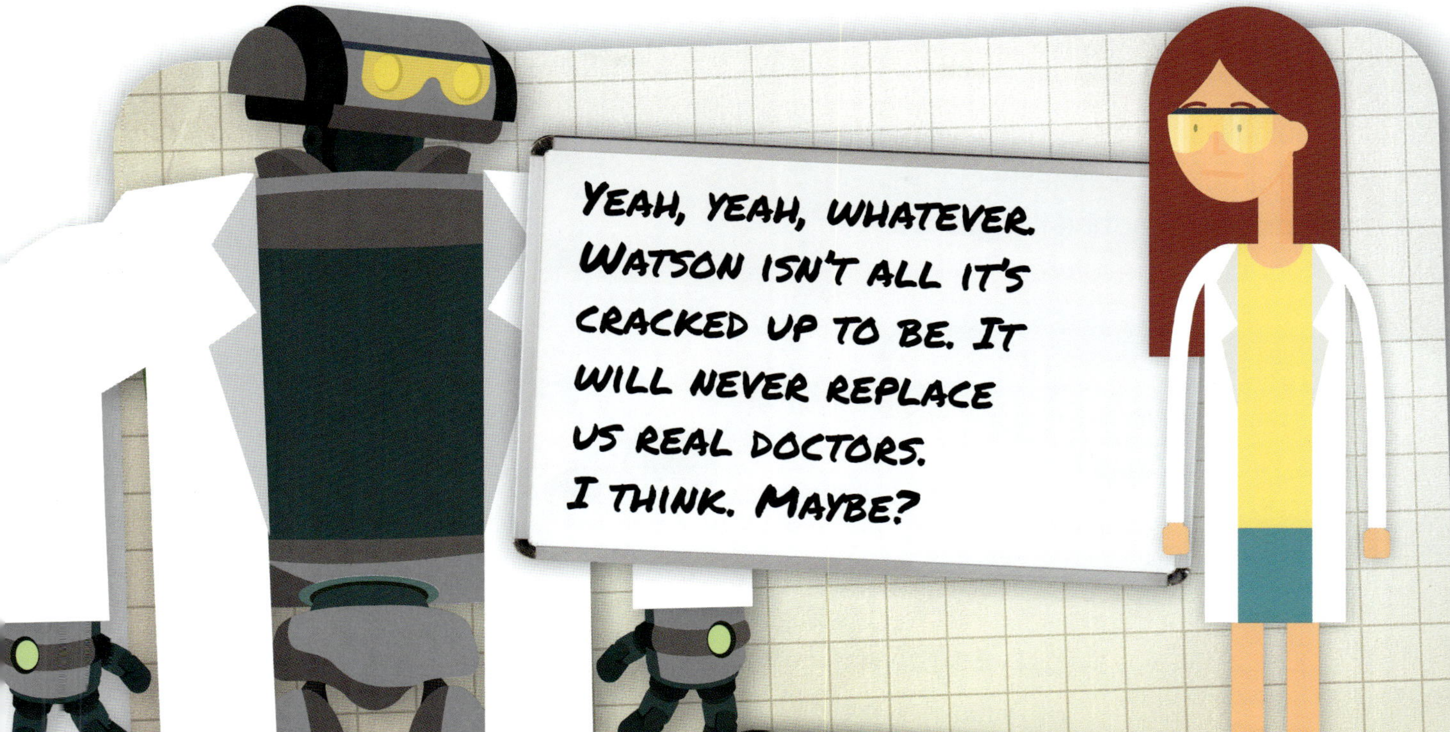

Watson is capable of learning much more information than a real doctor, and much faster too. In a similar way to the chatbots, Watson may be used to listen to a patient's problems and then use its huge amount of medical information to tell the patient what is wrong. Watson may also be used to pick out the most important bits of information from textbooks and give this to the doctors. This would save the doctors lots of time.

AN EARLY PROTOTYPE OF WATSON

WHEN RECOMMENDING TREATMENT FOR CANCER PATIENTS, DOCTORS AGREED WITH WATSON 99% OF THE TIME.

Unfortunately, Watson isn't so useful when treating patients with rarer diseases, because there isn't much information available on those diseases. However, as AI continues to get better, computer programmers in the future may be able to create an even more powerful medical AI than Watson.

NANOTECHNOLOGY

Nanotechnology is all about objects smaller than 100 nanometers. Nanotechnology is used in medicine today, and it is going to be very important in the future.

A NANOMETER IS A BILLIONTH OF A METER. A HUMAN HAIR IS AROUND 100,000 NANOMETERS THICK.

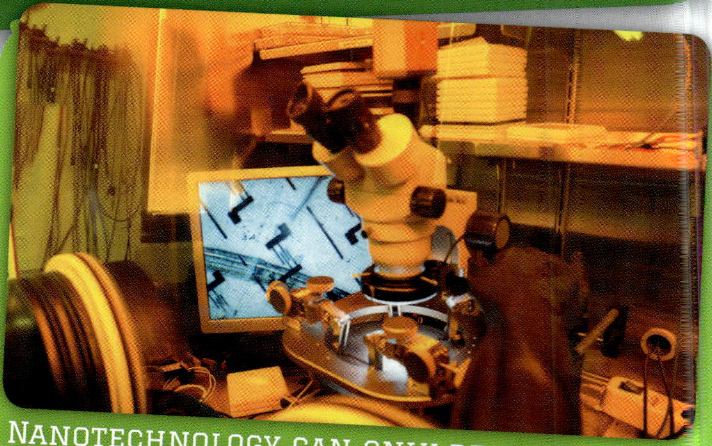

NANOTECHNOLOGY CAN ONLY BE SEEN WITH POWERFUL ***MICROSCOPES.***

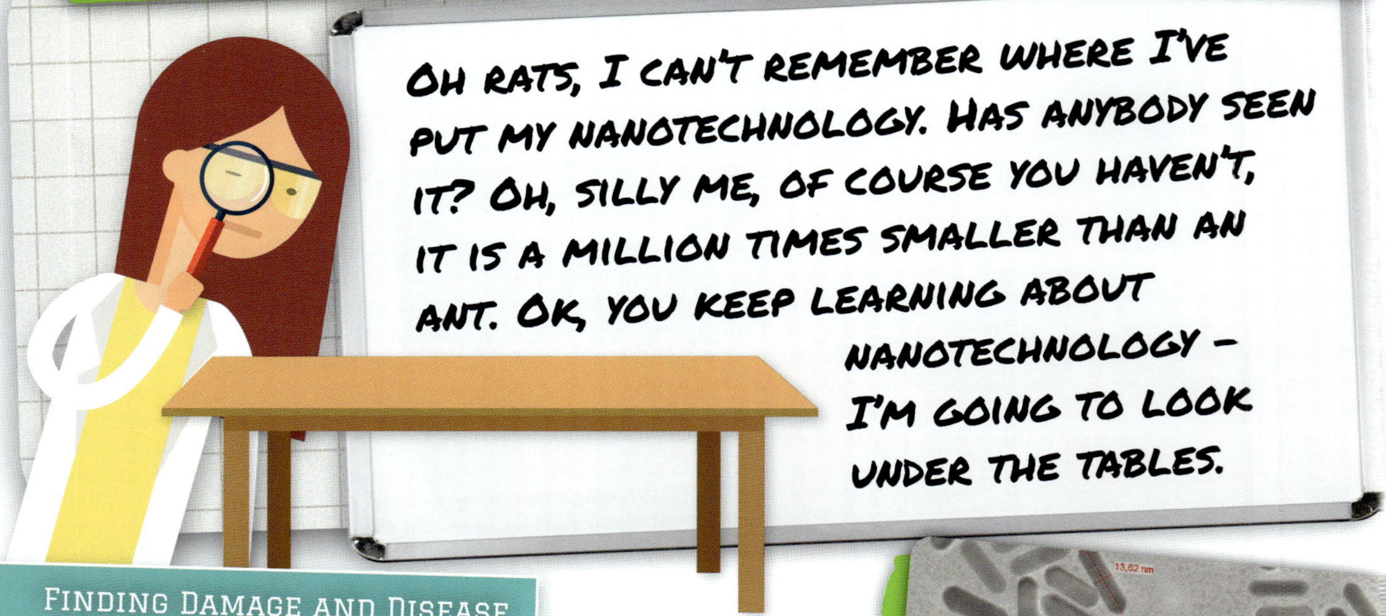

FINDING DAMAGE AND DISEASE

Gold ***NANORODS*** can be used to ***DETECT*** injury and disease. Here's how they detect kidney injury:

- SCIENTISTS CREATE NANORODS THAT ARE FULL OF HOLES. THESE HOLES ARE SHAPED LIKE THE PROTEINS FOUND IN DAMAGED KIDNEYS.
- THE NANORODS ARE ADDED TO URINE FROM THE PATIENT'S BODY.
- IF THERE ARE ANY KIDNEY-INJURY PROTEINS IN THE URINE, THEY WILL FIT IN THE NANOROD'S HOLES LIKE A JIGSAW.
- A LIGHT IS SHONE ON THE NANOROD. THE NANOROD SHINES A DIFFERENT COLOR IF IT HAS PICKED UP ANY KIDNEY-INJURY PROTEINS.
- THE DOCTORS NOW KNOW IF THERE IS A PROBLEM WITH THE PATIENT'S KIDNEY.

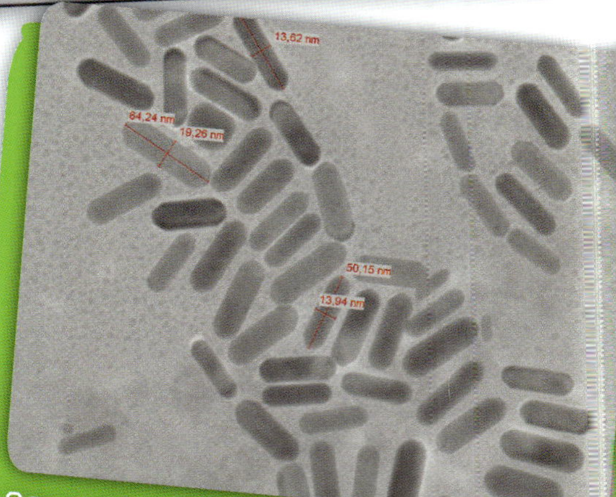

GOLD NANORODS UNDER A MICROSCOPE

Cancer Bombs

Nanotechnology is also useful for treating cancer. Cancer is caused by cells that do not do what they are supposed to. These cells create tumors, which are growths inside the body. Tumors can be dangerous, especially if they get in the way of organs and stop them doing their job properly.

Currently, cancer is treated using chemotherapy. In chemotherapy, the body is given drugs that are good at destroying tumors, but that also damage the rest of the body, making the person very ill. However, using nanotechnology, tiny nanoparticles could be attached to the tumors themselves. The nanoparticles would deliver the chemotherapy drugs to the cancer cells only, leaving the rest of the body unharmed.

More Nanotechnology under a Microscope

SOME NANOPARTICLES DON'T TREAT CANCER CELLS BY DELIVERING DRUGS – INSTEAD THEY ARE HEATED BY LASERS UNTIL THEY EXPLODE! BECAUSE THE NANOPARTICLES ARE SO SMALL, THE EXPLOSION ONLY DAMAGES THE CANCER CELLS.

iKNIFE

The iKnife is a piece of technology that can tell a surgeon if a piece of tissue is cancerous or not. Currently, it is hard for surgeons to know what tissue is cancerous when they are **OPERATING** on a patient, because cancerous and noncancerous tissue looks the same. This means that tissue may have to be sent to a laboratory if they are not sure, and this can take a long time. Sometimes, not all the cancerous tissue is removed in the first operation, meaning the cancer will come back and the patient will need surgery again.

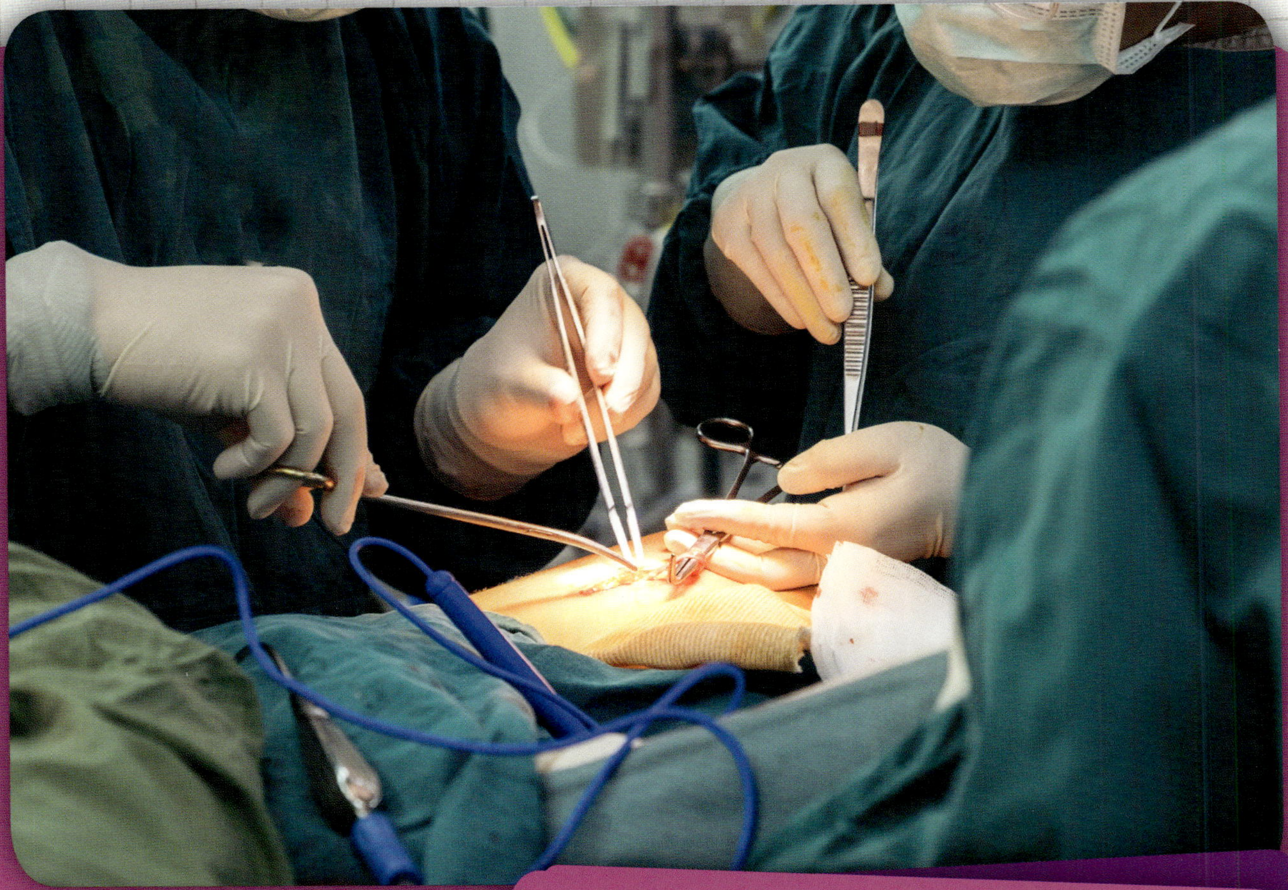

SURGERY

WHEN TESTED, THE iKNIFE HAS BEEN CORRECT 100% OF THE TIME SO FAR.

ELECTRIC KNIVES

Cancer surgery might become very different with the iKnife. It only takes the iKnife a few seconds to tell the surgeon if a piece of tissue is cancerous. This makes the operation much quicker, and it is easier for the surgeon to make sure there is no cancerous tissue left in the patient.

How Does the iKnife Work?

The iKnife uses electricity to heat the blade up. As the iKnife cuts into the tissue, smoke is released because of the heat. The smoke is detected by a spectrometer, which is a piece of technology that can tell what the smoke is made up of. If there are signs of cancer in the smoke, the spectrometer tells the surgeon that the tissue needs to be removed.

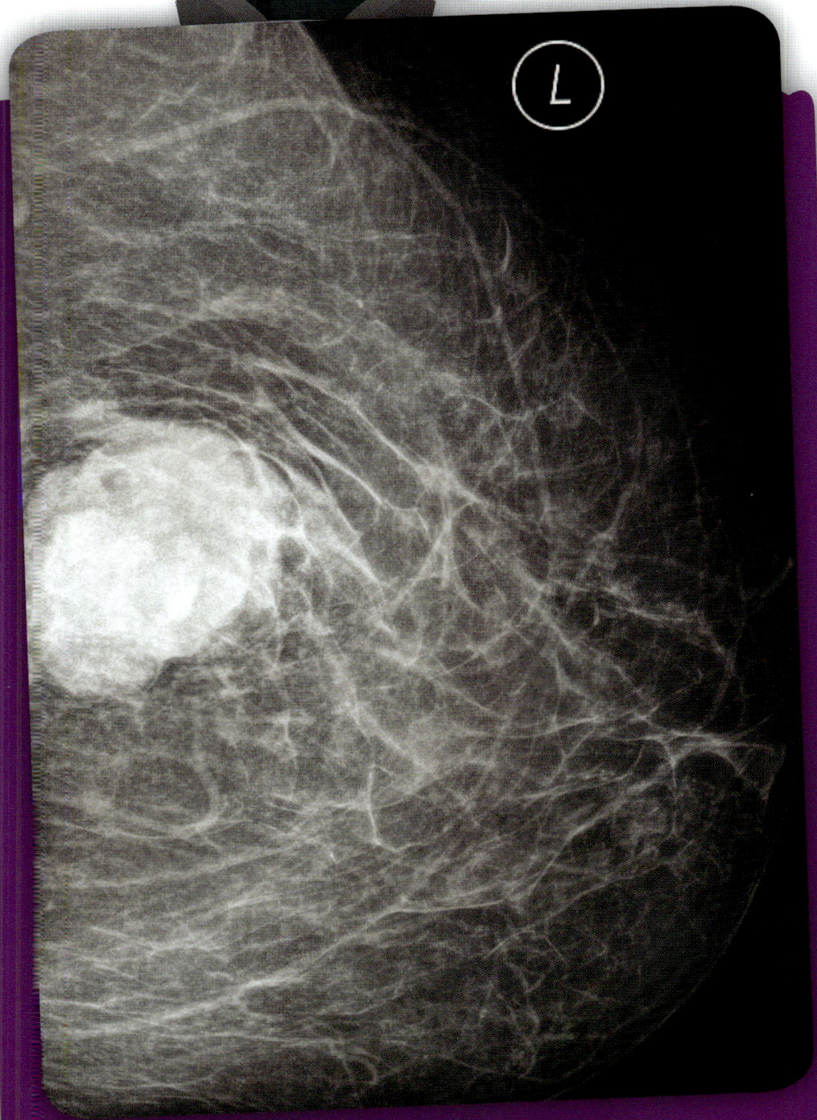

An image showing cancer in white

Because cancer is such a serious disease, doctors around the world are very excited about the iKnife. However, the iKnife can detect other things as well. It can also tell what kind of germs are inside the tissue, or if the tissue is getting enough blood.

Super-high-tech-electrically-heated-intelligent knives? Awesome! I'll take four!

THE FUTURE OF STEM IN MEDICINE

CHANGING THE WORLD ISN'T EASY, YOU KNOW. WE ARE GOING TO NEED LOTS OF SMART NEW SCIENTISTS, ENGINEERS, AND MATHEMATICIANS IN THE FUTURE. HERE ARE SOME OF THE THINGS THAT THEY MIGHT BE WORKING ON...

NANOROBOTS

While today's nanotechnology is all about nanoparticles and nanorods, in the future we may have nanorobots. These will be tiny robots programmed to do all sorts of things. One day, nanorobots may even be injected into our **BLOODSTREAM** to detect diseases and help us get better. Hundreds of years in the future, nanorobots may be able to move and rearrange atoms. This means they could change and build whatever we want.

NANOROBOTS

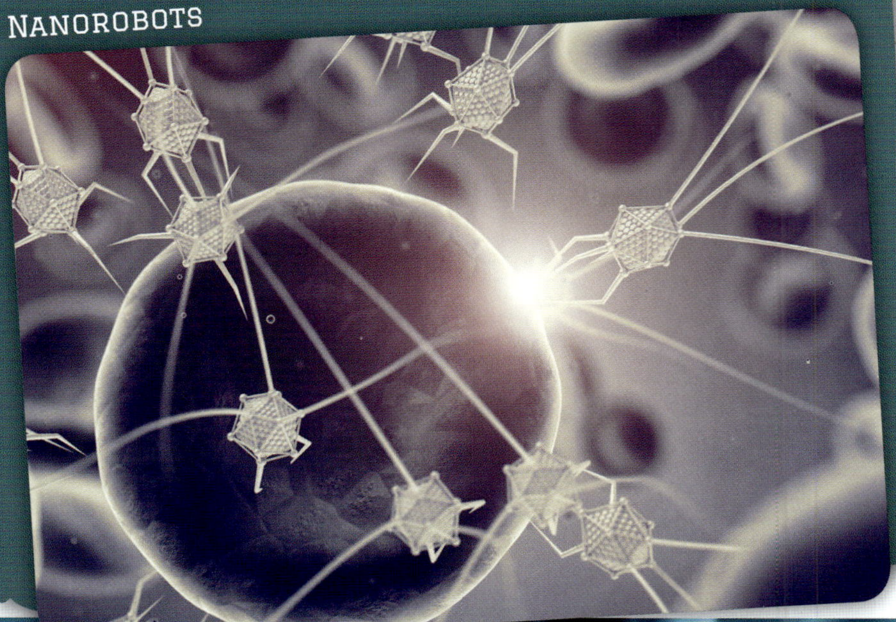

Apps

In the future, visits to the doctor may be replaced with apps instead. Apps of the future might be programmed with AI to help us stay healthy and prevent disease. Much like Watson, the app would ask us questions and use lots of medical information to tell us what is wrong. The app may also use technology to measure things, like our heart rate. Then the app would tell you how to stay healthy, or if you need to visit the doctor.

APPS ON PHONES MAY HELP US STAY HEALTHY.

Virtual Brains

Do you remember the lab-grown organoids that teach scientists about disease? Scientists and programmers are also working on creating a virtual, computer brain. By looking at the effects of virtual diseases on the virtual brain, scientists will be able to learn what might happen to a real brain.

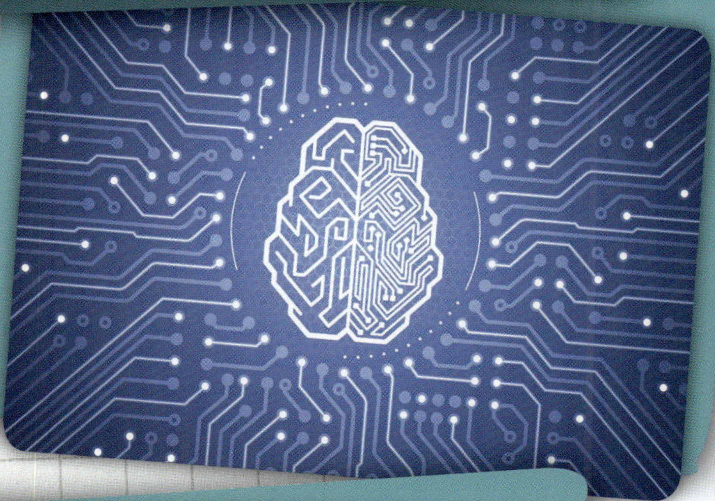

SOME SCIENTISTS THINK THAT ONE DAY IT WILL BE POSSIBLE TO PUT OUR MINDS INTO A VIRTUAL BRAIN AND LIVE FOREVER.

HOME TIME

THERE'S THE BELL. IT LOOKS LIKE ANOTHER DAY IN STEM SCHOOL HAS COME TO AN END. I'VE GOT TO GO – I NEED TO FINISH BUILDING MY ROBOT ARMY. UM, I MEAN ARM! ROBOT ARM. NOT ARMY. NO, NO. NOTHING TO SEE HERE. ANYWAY, IF YOU LIKE STEM AND WANT TO LEARN MORE, THEN READ ON...

FIND OUT MORE

You could see if your school has any after school STEM programs. Try talking to your teacher or your parents about how to get involved in STEM. You could also try thinking like a scientist, mathematician, or engineer yourself! STEM is all about solving problems – next time you see a problem, think about how it can be solved. You might be able to test your idea and see if it works. That is what STEM is all about.

FOLLOW THESE LINKS TO KEEP ON LEARNING ONLINE:

SCIENCE EXPERIMENTS
– www.funology.com/science-experiments/

BBC SCIENCE
– http://www.bbc.co.uk/education/subjects/z6svr82

CRASHCOURSE SCIENCE VIDEOS
– www.youtube.com/user/crashcoursekids

GLOSSARY

3D an object which has height, width, and depth

ACIDS liquids that can break down objects into small pieces

ANTIBIOTIC a substance that stops bacteria from growing

ARTIFICIAL something that is human-made; not natural

BIOLOGICAL relating to living things

BLOODSTREAM the cycle of blood going around the body

CELLS the basic units that make up all living things

CHAMBERS closed spaces

CHEMICALS substances that materials are made from

DETECT to sense or record

ELECTRODES electric conductors used to transfer electricity to nonconductive materials

ENERGY power that is required for an activity

GEL a thick, jelly-like substance

LABORATORY a room or building used by scientists to conduct experiments and research

LESS ECONOMICALLY DEVELOPED COUNTRIES countries with a weaker economy

LIMBS an arm or leg, or the wings of birds

MATTER substances from which things are made

MICROSCOPES instruments used by scientists to see very small things

NANORODS rods or sticks that are less than 100 nanometers thick

NEURONS nerve cells

OPERATING performing surgery on a patient

SCALPELS small, sharp knives used by surgeons

SENSOR technology that can detect and record things

SURGEON a doctor who performs operations that involve cutting into someone's body to repair damage

SYSTEMS sets of things that work together to do specific jobs

TISSUE what organs and other body parts are made of

VACCINES a type of medicine that prevents other diseases and illnesses

VIRTUAL something that is simulated by computers, but does not exist in the real world

INDEX

PHOTO CREDITS

Front Cover – Puwadol Jaturawutthichai, xpixel, balabolka, Diana Taliun, paulista, Lipskiy, mayrum. 3 – Phonlamai Photo, Puwadol Jaturawutthichai, Africa Studio, Diana Taliun. 4 – volkovslava, Fun Way Illustration. 5 – DenisProduction.com, promtorg. 6 – Africa Studio, natalunata, Satirus. 7 – PowerUp, Rvector. 8 – Suttha Burawonk, Milagli. 9 – kaling2100, ktsdesign. 10 – byatalar, Fun Way Illustration, Master Video. 11 – Wikicommons. 12 – Diego Cervo, chombosan. 13 – Casa nayafana, Eakphum. 14 – sportpoint, Wikicommons. 15 – Willyam Bradberry. 16 – Sudowoodo, Designua, RedlineVector. 17 – martin81, Matej Kastelic. 18 – Kateryna Kon, Peter Kotoff. 19 – vchal, extender_01. 20 – Sky vectors, wsf-s. 21 – everytime, boscorelli. 22 – TZIDO SUN, Zapp2Photo. 23 – Fun Way Illustration, Wikicommons. 24 – Moreno Soppelsa, Wikicommons. 25 – GiottoDesign, Andrus Ciprian. 26 – Samrith Na Lumpoon. 27 – KANIVETS LIUDMYLA, Fun Way Illustration. 28 – nobeastsofierce. 29 – vectorfusionart, Sergey Tarasov. 30 – wavebreakmedia. Border on all pages: paulista. Graph Paper – The_Pixel. Tess Tube – mayrum. mages are courtesy of Shutterstock.com. With thanks to Getty Images, Thinkstock Photo and iStockphoto.